Always Skating Forward

Amazing Adults

Joanne Vassallo Jamrosz

Wasteland Press
www.wastelandpress.net
Shelbyville, KY USA

Always Skating Forward:
Amazing Adults
by Joanne Vassallo Jamrosz

First Printing – May 2019
ISBN: 978-1-68111-310-4

Printed in the U.S.A.

0   1   2   3   4   5   6   7

Adult Skaters,

May even your smallest trace always bring you joy

TABLE OF CONTENTS

ACKNOWLEDGMENTS

My heartfelt thanks to the following people who helped make *Always Skating Forward: Amazing Adults* a reality.

To Tim Renfrow and the wonderful staff at Wasteland Press for their publishing magic, for always being there when the questions fly, and for always having a ready answer. Also, I can't thank you enough for your beautiful cover designs. You always capture the spirit of our *Skating Forward* books.

For the staff at US Figure Skating, my Skating Magazine editor Troy Schwindt and my web page editor Taylor Dean for all your support and always willing to lend a hand with a research question. Especially a great big shout out to Karen Cover, Skating Museum curator who is a wealth of skating information.

For Lexi Rohner, Aviva Cantor and the wonderful adult skating committee. You are always available with a helpful answer and for your support of your adult skaters, and your help when they have questions.

For the Adult skating community. Your support, your camaraderie and your spirit not only inspire me every day but also inspire others.

For the very talented and inspiring U.S Championship Mens competitor Jordan Moeller. Thank you for your encouraging words and for a Foreword so beautifully written.

For my twelve amazing adults, Suzie, Kim C, Kim E, Heather, Ken, Castella, Christine, Tracy, Karen, Terryl, Aleli and Melissa. Thank you for taking time from your very busy lives to share a bit of yourself with our readers. Your stories not only inspire, they encourage as well. No doubt, because of your stories, I believe many adults will think about grabbing a pair of skates and hit the ice. Wouldn't that be wonderful?

Finally, for my Gregory. You are my biggest cheerleader and without a doubt, the greatest skating fan in our house. Thank you for attending every event with me, often sitting in a cold rink from dawn to dusk, always cheering. Thank you for being my cheerleader when deadlines loom, and final edits need completion. Most of all, for all the long hours you spend with me at book vendor events. You and our little April Mae are my whole world. I love you, and I thank you.

I'm so blessed and thankful to meet and work with the most incredible skaters through these very special *Skating Forward* books. I am so grateful to work with each and every one, to get to know them and to share a very special part of them with all of you. There are so many more skaters out there. So many more stories to tell, and tell them, we will.

With a grateful heart, I thank you.

Love and Blessings,
Joanne

FOREWORD

It is October 2, 2018. Earlier this evening, I learned of the untimely passing of my ice dance partner and friend, Ashleyann Carlson. I apologize for beginning on a solemn note but, without Ashleyann, I would not be part of the world of adult skating as I am now. I have only known Ashleyann for a few years, but she was one of the most kindhearted, passionate people I have ever had the good fortune of meeting. For the last two years, I had the opportunity to compete at Adult Championships in Partnered Dance at the Bronze level with Ashleyann. Training and competing with Ashleyann gave me a whole new perspective on the sport of figure skating in a way that allowed me to see the joy and passion for skating that can be so easily lost in the day-to-day training. My experiences with her are ones that I will take with me, not only through the rest of my career, but also through the rest of my life.

As I stated earlier, it was through Ashleyann that introduced me to the adult skating community. From the second I stepped into the adult community, I felt the warmest of welcomes. I have met so many adult athletes who inspire me every day with their love of the sport and their desire to better themselves every single day, both on and off the ice. Between Ashleyann, our coach, Doreen Denny, our training-mates, our competitors, and everyone else I have met due to my journey in adult skating, I have never met so many supportive, passionate and driven people in my life and, for that, I thank you.

I thank you for your never-ending support. I thank you for your undying passion, for your constant drive, but most importantly, I thank you for your continuous inspiration. My time in the adult skating community has taught me to never give up, to support and love those around me, and to always be true to myself. I am certain that I would not be the competitor, or person that I am today if it weren't for Ashleyann and the rest of the adult skating community.

I will leave you with this. No matter what your goal is, whether it is in life, skating, family, relationships, work, or anything else, wake up each morning and do what you love. Be true to yourself. Love yourself and those around you. For if you do, how can you fail?

Jordan Moeller
U.S Championship Mens Competitor

INTRODUCTION

A dult figure skaters have a motto and they are proud to shout it from the rooftops. "Adults Skate, too". Indeed, they do.

When I joined my "adult" skating class back in 1988, we learned the same Basic Skills as the younger skaters. There was no adult track, no adult tests, no adult moves or freestyle. Most of the adults turned to dance because that was what adults were "supposed" to do. Adult Championships? Well that was in the very beginning stages, and nothing like the phenomenal event it is today.

Fast forward to 2019. Look at adult skating today. Adult tests are abundant and so are adult competitions, so many, we couldn't list them all here. Adults, lookout. You now have sectional qualifiers, and nationals, well today appropriately named Championships. How fitting, because when I think of adult skaters, I think of champions. Amazing.

Over the years, so many adults were willing to share their stories in previous *Skating Forward* books. But always, always it was a dream of mine to create an adults only *Skating Forward* book that introduced some of the most inspiring skaters I ever met.

In 2014, my husband and I attended the Adult Championships in Hyannis, MA. *Always Skating Forward: Amazing Adults* began there. The seeds for this book planted when I watched the then Adult V skaters proudly take to the ice with the most amazing programs I had ever seen, Oh, and if you are not familiar with Adult V skaters, they are 66 plus in years.

When the competition ended, I went up to one of the ladies who just had the skate of her life and congratulated her. She just glowed in her purple and gold sparkly dress, purple boa and feather hat.

I told her how impressed I was and how inspiring she was! Her answer? "Honey, I don't think I'm inspiring. I'm 78 years old. This is what I love to do, and it sure beats sitting home in a rocking chair, dying by the day. If I have to grow old. I am growing old on the ice!"

Amen, Sister.

So it seems only fitting that our next *Skating Forward* book recognizes a group of skaters who are proud to call themselves adult skaters and so much more. I'm thrilled to introduce their stories.

A young woman who had a successful adult competitive career. Since then, she discovered her "voice" and now shines in community musical theater. Likewise, another competitor and instructor who spends her time off the ice playing in the pit orchestra for community musicals. A current adult medalist dedicates her days as teacher to her very happy and supportive first graders, and another young woman celebrates her time on ice teaching and competing with her synchro skaters because she is a proud cancer survivor.

Yes, adults skate, but unlike their young skating friends, they also skate while working nine to five jobs and 12 hour days, maintaining relationships with their spouses and partners, raising little ones, taking care of elderly parents and other life issues and in between, in between all of this, they find time to dedicate to the sport they love.

Adults don't just skate. Adults are skating, and they are skating every day. I am proud to introduce you to twelve amazing adults. Figure skating plays a major role in their everyday lives, and their off ice stories are also remarkable. I hope their inspiring stories will touch your heart and make you smile.

Always Skate Forward,
Joanne

Suzie Marie's Story

"If I am watching, reading or playing a character in a story I don't necessarily enjoy the perfect character because in life no one is perfect. I love a multi- faceted character or one who reveals their flaws and makes self realizations"
                                        –Suzie Marie Flynn

Former Adult Championships' competitor Suzie Marie Flynn is proud of the medals she won at this prestigious skating competition, bronze and pewter, but today, this vibrant young woman's place is on the stage in musical theater and as the new lead singer in the band Tunnels End.

Sunnycrest Skating Rink in Syracuse, NY is where Suzie Flynn first discovered the sport of figure skating.

"My father used to take us skating when I was just able to walk," Suzie remembers. "I used to take these tiny steps and one day I took forever to do this turn on the ice. I marched around in a circle threw my hands up in the air and yelled 'Linda

Fratianne!' My father was amazed because I was maybe about four years old," Suzie remembers.

Suzie's father was a member of the Air National Guard, and attended the 1980 Winter Olympic Games in Lake Placid.

"I must have been paying attention when my mother talked about my father being there. I don't remember but I'm assuming Linda Fratianne was on TV skating when my mother was talking about my father being at the Olympic Games."

Suzie began private lessons and competing at the age of 13, and since she was mostly self taught, the sport came easy. She competed in North Atlantic Regionals and Empire State Games and became the first skater in her club's history to earn a USFS gold medal in freestyle and moves in the field.

"This was a big deal when most skaters struggled to pass intermediate freestyle." She also holds medals in solo ice dancing, ice dancing and her 6th figures test.

"I traveled and trained at many centers on the East coast and worked with World and Olympic Coaches, and for a time in my twenties I actively searched for an ice dancing partner," Suzie explains.

At the time this focused young skater also competed in Adult Sectionals and Adult Championships as a 2007 national bronze and pewter medalist. She also won a bronze and pewter at the 2009 Adult Championships.

As much as she enjoyed skating, Suzie harbored another dream and secretly worked at it most of her life. She loved to sing, and she loved musical theater.

"Music was always part of our family," Suzie explains. "We started playing instruments when I was young. I was never very good about practicing. I tried flute and saxophone, but didn't enjoy them. What I did enjoy was singing and dancing."

It would be a special move to Virginia six years ago that brought Suzie to the stage, something she always dreamed about.

"Because of back problems I know I couldn't compete anymore. My aunt encouraged me to try out for *South Pacific*. I was hoping for a role in ensemble. I had auditioned for some local plays when I was younger, so I knew what it was like to be nervous and sing in front of a small group of people so close to you that you could hear their breathing, but I hadn't done it that often and was so nervous," Suzie explains.

The gracious director not only offered her a call back but also told her she narrowly missed the role of Nellie Forbush.

"She complimented me and said when I sang it was like pixie dust coming down. Wow. I was so surprised that people enjoyed my voice that much. Family always told me I sang well but they have to. They're family, right? But, for a stranger to tell me they loved listening to me sing gave me a great boost of confidence."

In 2017, this talented young woman won the role of a lifetime, and to this day, her most memorable role. Suzie won the lead, Dolly Levi, in the Castaways Repertory Theatre production of *Hello Dolly*.

"My favorite role was probably Dolly in *Hello Dolly*," Suzy exclaims. "This was such a great opportunity to not only lead a musical but to sing and dance! I had to sing a lead or solo for about 9 or 10 songs."

Thrilled with her new role in musical theater, Suzie also loved how determined the character of Dolly was, the sneaky ways she tried to get what she wanted.

"In the end she realizes she is in love and this self realization changes her into a softer, almost sweeter character. I also liked that she was an older character. If I am watching, reading or playing a character in a story I don't necessarily enjoy the perfect character because in life no one is perfect. I love a multifaceted character or one who reveals their flaws and makes self realizations."

The busy young woman remains active on stage and has since participated in over a dozen plays and musicals from playing Elaine in *Arsenic and Old Lace*, to Velma in *Hairspray* and Ethel in *The Music Man*. She also won the best actress award for her role in *Hello Dolly* at Castaways and won a supporting actress nomination for her role of Dina in *South Pacific*.

Like many musical theater performers, Suzie has a dream role in mind. Suzie would love to play Cassie in *A Chorus Line*, someday.

"Being that I am not a teenager or in my early twenties I can relate to the main character and her struggle to get back on stage," Suzie explains. "I like the complexity of the show and the raw feelings. What those characters describe is so like many people who struggle to make it in professional acting, singing, dancing and even figure skating, especially women looking for a figure skating partner. Just because you sacrifice doesn't mean you get the dream role or part. In the end, you have to love the performing and not be in love with stardom. The song "What I Did for Love" reminds me of the many sacrifices I've made in my life to be a competitive skater and coach."

Many of Suzie's skating experiences have helped shape her theater life today.

"My ability to pick up choreography, keep proper posture, add facial expressions and small body movement to make the moves unique, the work ethic, the confidence on stage and precision with movements all come from figure skating," Suzie explains.

She also offers plenty of good advice for anyone dreaming of attempting a stage role someday, from reading to following audition requirements.

"Make sure to give the director what he or she wants. If they want an upbeat song, don't go in singing a ballad. If they want a monologue try memorizing it and add movement."

Her other piece of advice?

"Don't take it personally. When you go to auditions sometimes, the director already knows whom they want. They've worked with people; know people and they have it stuck in their head what would make their vision come alive. Remember we are different people and look at things with different eyes and ears. What we see at audition and we think would be good in a role isn't necessarily the same as the person sitting next to you or the director in charge of everything."

She also stresses the importance of reflection.

"Even if you thought you were perfect for a role what could you have done better at an audition?" Suzie advises. "Did you choose a song that demonstrates your abilities? This is a mistake I often make I don't always choose songs that show a good range, yet I am mezzo soprano with the ability to sing alto and high notes. Sometimes we just need to take time because we get disappointed when rejected. So step away, take a week, then reflect to see what you can do better."

And if you love theater and want to be more involved take ensemble roles or help back stage.

"If you want them to see your work ethic, dependability and what you can do, be in the ensemble. Show them you are easy to work with and your singing and dancing abilities."

This determined young woman knows the importance of keep trying to reach your dream, and pursuing what you love to do, no matter what. Suzie recently began singing with the band Tunnels End.

"Currently I am living my dream," explains the happy new singer. "I am officially their lead female singer and couldn't be more thrilled. I have wanted to sing with a band for years. But it was hard to break into. I didn't have a lot of connections and some bands couldn't get past my lack of experience with equipment and the fact that most of my singing is musical theater. All of a sudden, I started getting auditions, feast or famine, and the band I really wanted to be in Tunnels End, finally chose me."

For this dedicated woman who found success as an adult skater, musical theater performer and lead band singer, pursuing that singing dream was worth of every second.

"They are the nicest bunch of guys," she says of her fellow band members who love to play pop, rock and classic rock. "They are so much fun to watch and listen to them play, and now they have me," states a proud Suzie.

Tracy's Story

"A moment that will once again live in me, forever. These women didn't even know me when my journey started, yet here they are helping me celebrate, some of them not even knowing how big this anniversary was. It was a wonderful surprise and a reminder that I am not alone."

–Tracy Blomquist

Tracy Blomquist's skating moments involves team work and team work only. Tracy is a proud member of the Starlights Synchronized Adult Team in Chicago, IL, and this very driven and inspirational skater will tell you it is her synchro team skating and teammates that got her through the most devastating of diagnoses. Cancer.

Growing up, Tracy suffered from a painful condition called endometriosis. It's a condition of the reproductive system and it can cause abdominal scarring and adhesions as well as ovarian cysts and other issues.

"There are days when the pain was so bad, I am not sure how I got out of bed," Tracy recalls. "At times it was challenging to train because I was in so much pain but I pushed myself. I wasn't officially diagnosed until college when I finally had my first surgery. I had another surgery four years later. While those surgeries helped it is something I will struggle with the rest of my life."

This brings Tracy to the biggest challenge she would face.

"In January of 2012, my doctor ordered some extra tests because some things didn't seem right," continues Tracy. "I went through the biopsy and waited for the results. My doctor seemed assured it was nothing but with my history we wanted to rule anything out."

The morning of January 9, 2012, Tracy woke up with a bad feeling she couldn't shake. Later that morning she would get the call no one wants to receive. She answered the phone when her doctor called.

"She was a bubbly personality and I could tell something was wrong because her tone was different. I don't remember much of what she said but I do remember she said 'I have your results and I am sorry it came back showing carcinoma'."

Tracy's head was spinning as she was writing down the oncologists name she was to contact to learn her treatment protocol.

"I had no idea what I was going to do next. Was I going to lose my hair? Do I have to have radiation? What was the surgery going to be like? Am I going to be able to have kids? Am I going to die? I was only 33 years old."

Tracy also remembers her synchro team leaving for a competition that same week, on Friday morning.

"I was hoping to get an appointment before I left town but I had to wait another two weeks," remembers Tracy.

Tracy told just a few close teammates what was happening, and she actually looked forward to leaving town and going to her happy place, the ice.

"As my friends and I call it, the bubble. You enter the bubble, competition weekend and forget everything at home, and just skate. When the weekend is over, the bubble pops and you get back to the real world and life. Ha!"

That weekend Tracy was hoping for a great team skate and a moral victory.

"We had a terrible skate and placed last, but I was thankful I got to escape my situation for a few days and skate with my friends," Tracy gratefully remembers.

When Tracy finally met with her oncologist, he sent her slides out for review and did another biopsy himself. The doctor confirmed her cancer was in the early stages, and recommended a hysterectomy as treatment, but also gave her a fertility saving option since she was unmarried and wanted to have children.

"So I opted for that and scheduled my surgery for a few weeks later. It was a stressful time. I was in school completing my advanced imaging degrees, working full time and performing clinical rotations at night and coaching skating. I informed my team and coaches as to what was going on. Since it was middle season, I was not certain if I could skate Nationals. They were all so great."

But this determined young woman was NOT going to keep away from the ice.

Tracy's surgery took place on February 9, 2012. She was not allowed to work or skate for a few weeks, but felt well enough to attend her team's practice the following Sunday.

"What I walked into would change my life forever. I walked into the rink and as I am saying hello to everyone, I see they are wearing teal and white (the color of cervical cancer). I then realized that the senior team was also decked out this way. I was blown away."

Tracy notes that cancer is a humbling experience and people often don't know what to say.

"It can be very isolating as well," she acknowledges. "The amount of love and support I felt that morning was just extraordinary. These women will never truly understand what that moment meant to me. Everyone processes cancer differently. I personally felt I wanted to be a voice and educate others. Cancer can happen to any of us, even the healthiest appearing people. One week later I was able to tell the team that the doctor was able to get all the cancer and I was cancer free."

Nationals were just a few weeks away and Tracy was unsure if she would be able to skate.

"But I knew I was going to be there no matter what and whatever capacity," says a determined Tracy. "I was able to jump back into the program the weekend before we left. We had our send off exhibition and people were so happy to see me back on the ice and with the team."

Tracy still had some issues with stitches and knew she had to be as cautious as possible, but nothing was going to keep her from skating, especially cancer.

"We did not have a great skate and ended up 9th. Everyone was quiet in the locker room when my friend Lisa said, 'Hey guys, at least we beat cancer!' That broke the tension in the locker room and everyone laughed and cried. She was right. We beat cancer. Skating was my therapy and I am not sure how my fight would have been different if skating wasn't back in my life."

For the next three years, Tracy had checkups at three month intervals to make sure the cancer was gone and stayed gone. There were a few bumps in the road, and a few scares but her teammates continued to be there for her and cheer her on.

"I was just counting the days until five years cancer free, because the likelihood of reoccurrence is greatly reduced then. As I continued to skate each year on or around February 9, we would create my Cancerversary and wear teal. Around my 5th anniversary I went with a few of my teammates to get a tattoo of a teal and white ribbon to celebrate 5 years. I was also competing that weekend and again to my surprise the whole team had matching shirts on that said 'Five Years Strong'."

This amazing young woman keeps inspiring her teammates and the people she works with everyday. When she is not on the ice, Tracy works in radiology at an Orthopedic Group in Chicago, as the lead MRI- CT technologist.

"I love working in orthopedics and I also get to take care of professional athletes as the doctors I work for take care of the Chicago Bulls basketball team and the Chicago White Sox baseball and Chicago Fire soccer teams. I always wanted to work with athletes or a professional team and this has given me the opportunity to do so."

Most of all she is grateful she returned to skating back in Cleveland, Ohio in 2004 and immediately joined adult synchronized skating. That love for team skating continues today with her team in Chicago.

"What motivates me to get on the ice is the thrill of competition," states a proud Tracy. "It's your opportunity to show what you have been working so hard on all season. There's nothing better than the adrenaline of competition. You won't win them all but you got out there and tried."

For Tracy believes whether you skate your entire life, start as an adult or come back to the ice after years away, skating is a sport like no other.

"Skaters have drive, tenacity mental toughness and fight! We push ourselves mentally, physically and emotionally. We all fall down and all get back up. We win some, we lose some, but it is the friendships I have made and continue to make through skating. They are special friendships because we all understand how this sport has shaped the women and men we've become now. We have an even bigger love and appreciation for the sport and each other."

It was that support and her teammate's love that got this special young woman through the darkest time of her life.

"These women didn't even know me when my journey started, yet there they are helping me celebrate, some of them not even knowing how big an anniversary this was. It was a wonderful surprise and a reminder that I am not alone."

Ken's Story

"It was such an emotional and symbolic gesture and I cried when I read the post. It reminded me, this is why I continue to compete as an adult skater, because of the memories we create and the friendships we forge. And like the paper flowers, they last forever."

–Ken Ho

Adult skaters dream of coming home with that special medal from the U.S. Adult Championships. They also hope to come home with another special memento. A Ken Ho paper flower.

Ken is an academic physician and assistant professor at the University of Pittsburgh. He is also a proud and successful adult competitor since the 2008 U.S. Adult Championships in Lake

Placid. It is his very special "tossies", however, that are what people most recognize and yearn to receive at each nationals.

"Someone once bought me these paper flower kits from a store as a present and I started making them because I like crafts in general," Ken recalled. "The first ones were awful, a misshapen disaster. They looked like birds' nests! But as I practiced more they started to resemble real flowers."

Ken also realized that he didn't have to continue buying the kits, which ran anywhere from 12 to 15 dollars. Color cardstock worked just as well, so he purchased that in several colors, and some wire, and he was off to the races.

"Then I could craft the flowers in any color I wanted," Ken says.

Around this time, the tossie wave at Adult Championships began. "People were throwing bags of candy, towels, tissues, stuffed animals and fresh flowers onto the ice. I thought to myself, people throw fresh flowers on the ice why don't I throw paper flowers? At least they would last longer."

So began Ken's personal and special tossies.

"I think the original flowers were first debuted at the Adult Nationals in Hyannis Port," remembers Ken. "These were just simple paper flowers without any adornments, bells or whistles."

Ken likes to match a flower to a skater (very reminiscent of the wands of Harry Potter). He has since added rhinestones to the edges of the flowers, and is always on the prowl for Swarovski Crystal discounts.

"The year that Nationals was held in North Carolina the flowers were all rainbow colored to raise awareness of the bathroom laws discriminating against transgender people," Ken continued. "One of my skating friends even asked me to craft flowers for her wedding which is an incredible honor for me. I usually craft over a hundred flowers per year to give to people. One year I would like to have one to give to every single person."

Ken is proud to say that many people keep their special Ken flowers. Some go through great lengths to protect them on their journey home. Others look like they've been loved a little more. Some people hang them at work. Some people put them in a vase at home.

"One year a Facebook thread emerged where everyone posted pictures of paper flowers that I made over the year," Ken proudly states. "It was such an emotional and symbolic gesture and I cried as I read the post. It reminded me that this is why I continue to compete as an adult skater. Because of the memories we create and the friendships we forge. And like the paper flowers, they last forever."

Ken of course, loves to take to the ice, and compete himself. He has a host of special skates at various Adult Championships, and smiles to think that this wonderful sport began for him, from a simple college PE class.

"I went to school in Ithaca, NY where it was cold much of the year and there were a lot of rinks," he says. "I was supposed to sign up for the paramedic class, yes that was offered as a physical education class at my college, but it was full, so my best friend said, 'Well you'll just have to take figure skating with me'."

Join the class he did, learning one foot spins and waltz jumps in the first week.

"In my mind I was so excited to be spinning and jumping, just like on TV, I thought."

Ken's first Adult Championships were in Lake Placid in the Silver Mens event.

"My coach couldn't make it that year and I was virtually petrified with anxiety," explains Ken, "I spent the six hours before I skated curled up in a bathroom stall. My other half refused to let me compete without a coach ever again. We took a break for a few years and I resumed competing in 2011 this time with my coach."

And this time at the Gold level.

His most memorable skates? Well, that's an easy one for Ken.

In 2017, a now Masters Intermediate- Novice Ken skated to a medley of songs from *Dirty Dancing* including the very popular "Time of My Life".

"At the 2017 Adult Nationals I took a heavy fall on an already injured knee, during a practice session the day before and was worried I would have to withdraw," Ken recalls. "I spent the rest of the day in bed with a bag of ice and a bottle of ibuprofen staring at a medal, a "tossie" that was given to me by Terryl with an inscription that read, 'For your passion to skate, and your courage to compete'."

That inscription was just the perfect encouragement this competitive adult skater needed.

"The next day I went out, had a good warm up and put out a skate that was good enough for the gold in the open event. This was my first gold medal at the Masters Intermediate Level. I then competed at the larger Championship level with the same program and had a passable but flawed program and it was good enough for 6th," Ken states.

Ken found himself sidelined for several months after this competition due to swelling from the injury. An MRI showed a bruised tendon, a partially torn meniscus and a ruptured Baker's cyst in the knee.

In 2018, Ken began competing once again, this time with a new program.

"But then weeks before Nationals I decided to resurrect the original program for the larger Championship level," Ken explains. "It felt very comfortable even after not having skated it for several months."

For the Championship event, Ken's parents, their friends and Ken's best friend Lanna flew in to watch him skate.

"I stepped on the ice for that performance and it was like the stars aligned and I went through each element cleanly one after the next. While I was doing 60's style dances that are part of the choreography, I saw the judges laughing and smiling. It was all over in a flash and the crowd was cheering and I was smiling so hard I was crying," says a proud Ken.

To accomplish this performance after months of injury cheered on by his family, friends and skating family meant the world to Ken.

"I took home a big Championship silver medal from this performance and it was my first time on the Championships podium. This was my most magical moment on ice," exclaims Ken.

He would also like to encourage other adults to give skating a try, and promises the benefits will be plenty both on and off the ice.

"There is a certain unspoken and unconditional love that is shared by the skating community," Ken says. "Your audience may be made up of friends, strangers and even your fellow competitors, but they are all your family. If you land your jump, they will cheer for you. If you fall, they will cheer for you more. In my book every person who has the courage to step on the ice and skate around on a 5mm of steel is a champion."

Karen's Story

"No matter how accomplished someone is in their personal life, the people I meet always seem very humble and down to earth when skating. I feel very blessed to be in this sport because it has brought so much to my life"

–Karen Viel

Who would have thought summer camp would be so much fun? If you're an adult skater and attended the Lake Tahoe High Sierra Adult Skate Camp in beautiful South Lake Tahoe you have some wonderful skating memories. This very special camp is all thanks to adult skater Karen Viel who proudly organized the camp for the past seven years.

"The first year we had 14 participants, 3 local coaches and 1 guest coach," Karen recalls. "This past May was our 7thyear, and we had 60 participants, 1 local coach and 11 guest coaches!"

This dedicated lady is also proud to tell you that she herself returned to adult skating at 52 years old, after taking a 27 year break from the sport, to raise her family.

"I have a gold medal in adult dance and adult free dance. I competed a little as an adult and competed in Championship

Dance in 2013 at US Adult Nationals. The commute to skate with a coach/partner is too expensive and prohibitive time wise to try and compete even though Adult Nationals was a very fun event."

Nonetheless, this lady is extremely supportive of the adult skating community, and the sport loved since she was eight years old.

"My parents gave me skating lessons for my birthday when I was eight years old," remembers Karen. "I immediately fell in love with it. I skated constantly and it was not only something I did to improve but it also became most of my social life. The freedom of movement and being on the ice is very special."

When Karen returned to skating as an adult, her goal was to get her gold medal in dance (back injuries made her give up jumping). She wanted to achieve this goal before reaching 60.

"I felt very fortunate to make a great new (now one of my best friends) friend who lives in Redwood City, CA, five minutes from the rink my coach was teaching at. She opened her home to me. This allowed me to make trips to skate with a coach a lot more affordable. I was able to not only pass my gold compulsory tests, but also the adult gold free dance and compete in Championship Dance at the 2013 Adult Nationals by the time I was 59," chimes a proud Karen.

Karen can't pin point one magical moment on ice, but rather many moments when skating touched her life in just the right way.

"As a kid I was able to participate in the Sun Valley Skating School one summer. There was a competition at the end of the summer and I really did not enjoy anything about that. However, we got to skate in the Saturday night shows every week and I absolutely loved that. I decided after that summer that my goal was to be able to skate in an ice show," Karen beams.

She proudly joined the Ice Capades after her second year of college.

Skating has always been a very special part of Karen's life. Family life growing up was not ideal, but certainly not miserable.

"We always had food, a roof over our head, although one of my stepsister's and I are always amazed how my mother managed, when we look back. I truly think skating helped me through all of our ups and downs growing up. When I was at the rink I concentrated on what I was trying to do skating wise and my friends were there."

As an adult, skating served as a similar outlet for a chosen career that sometimes proves stressful, but when skating Karen doesn't have time to think about it.

"I need to concentrate on my skating in order not to fall and crack my head again like I did a month after I started back," Karen now remembers with a grin. "For a few hours I am able to think of nothing but skating. Learning new dances, the Internationals, now challenge my brain and keep me more alert and keep me working."

She also credits her skating family who mean the world to her.

"Now that we have social media it is easy to reconnect and keep in touch with skating friends from my childhood, from Ice Capades and the skating friends I made from the camps I organize, camps and dance weekends I participate in, and all the great people I meet just by skating at different rinks."

Karen believes skaters share bonds that connect everyone.

"We know a lot of the same people we share similar experiences and we have a passion for skating that keeps us bonded," explains Karen. "Skating, even if not at the same level we would all love to be at is something we can potentially enjoy into our senior years. Richard Dwyer is a perfect example. A number of my family and friends commented that they wished they had something that they were passionate about. They feel like they are always searching for what will keep them focused and interested in life in their more mature years."

Karen happily spends her days in beautiful Lake Tahoe NV (Incline Village) on the Northeast corner of Lake Tahoe. Her 34 year old son works in software support. Daughter Sharisse is a writer and photographer.

"I've been fortunate enough to hire her as our photographer to take pictures at our Tahoe Adult Skate Camp," says this proud mom.

Sharisse is also married to a musician, Lee Coulter and is the mom of a happy ten year old son.

"Of course as all grandparents say about their grandkids, he is very awesome. I started taking him skating on my last couple of visits and he absolutely loves it," continues Karen.

This dedicated adult skater would love to encourage other adults to think about grabbing a pair of skates and hitting the ice.

"The most obvious answer is that it is a great form of fun exercise," Karen says. "As adults, we are not worried about how we compare with other people. We just want to continue to improve for our own self and have fun. It is a challenge both to our bodies and our brains, which they say helps keep our memory better for longer. I really hope that is the case."

She also notes another observation.

"Skaters seem to look younger than their chronological age most of the time. It's a great way to meet new people and be part of a very supportive group of people who have very diverse backgrounds and interests."

There are so many reasons why Karen Viel loves her sport.

"The feel of freedom when you are on the ice. The camaraderie of other skaters no matter what their accomplishments or levels. The exercise and how it makes me feel after I skate, knowing it is something I can do, wherever I go, and I will always make new friends."

Oh yes, and the friends.

"No matter how accomplished someone is in their personal life the people I meet always seem very humble and down to earth when skating," Karen says "I feel very blessed to be in this sport because it has brought so much to my life."

Castella's Story

"Poems and the paper are always there for me
Waiting for my next burst of emotions experiencing
Life's events to occur and just vent everything out
Until I feel satisfied with words spewing out the
Effervescent bubbling emotions so pent up inside
I need to keep working on creating more and feeling
Less ashamed but I always feel the need to be tamed
For there is a price pretty privilege protecting
Those who fall in the line's of the shapes society
Wants to make as I (constantly) tear at the wake of being
Woke I want to just soak up all this new information
And have it be a part of the new integration of the
Millennials first generation of newborn folk to lead
    greater lives
Push past more potential
Who said creativity couldn't be a way to reclamation and
    freedom

Let your words and heart ring
You always deserve to sing
About being yourself"

–Castella Copeland

C astella Copeland is still another adult skater, actively and happily competing at the Adult Gold level, but also sharing her time and talent with her very special Learn to Skate students.

This dedicated adult skater will be the first to tell you that sharing her love of skating with her students is just an added and special part of her skating experience.

Castella teachers at the Veterans Memorial Skating Rink in West Hartford, CT and at the International Skating Center in Simsbury, CT.

"I teach Learn to Skate at both rinks and teach folks of all ages and levels from Snowplow Sam up to Freestyle 6," Castella explains.

Castella has assisted in helping students with skills as well, such as moves in the field patterns or skills, for a test track, but generally teaches at her current level.

"The youngest student I have taught is two, and the oldest student I taught was 65 years old. I started teaching in 2008, and have loved teaching ever since."

What do this coach and adult skater love most about teaching? The word is connection.

"I love to connect with folks of all ages, backgrounds, sexualities, races and genders and learning abilities. We learn more about one another, the sport and ourselves as we progress through the skills. Diversity makes it fun," Castella explains.

"Diversity is the lived experience of difference in culture from the standard Anglo Normative practice. My life has consisted of being a multiracial female facing stigmatization about what it means to a true American citizen. I have learned how the stratification of society has formed standards surrounding heteronormativity, European culture, and masculinity that systematically deconstruct and devalue other cultures. My existence continues to challenge these standards since I do not fall under any of these standards. Though I have experienced privileges from time to time on a few axes of my identity, I have learned that it is the combination of all of my intersecting identities that makes me who I am today.

Understanding how my identity interacts with the larger role of diversity has allowed me to have a unique experience with social justice from a variety of perspectives. Having an intersectional mindset and approach has enabled me to question, learn, and advocate for the voices that are overheard and underrepresented.

Overall, my life has encompassed the multiculturalism of the core issues within social justice. Though many see these as obstacles or a burden, I see my differences classified as a minority to find solutions to these injustices. My journey began the day I was born; shaping me into a variety of characters that not only had to learn from trial and error but through the pain of not meeting the societal standards. Through the chapters of my life, I have grown into many different characters that have shaped me into who I am today never forgetting and growing from where I once was. Knowing this I bring unique experiences always seeking to be someone greater than who I was yesterday," Castella says.

For Castella it is amazing to watch her skaters not only grown and develop within the sport but also learn more about whom they are growing into outside of skating.

"I really enjoy having moments where I make a metaphor they can connect to via another sport or interest and then the student is able to understand the skill better and how to improve upon it," Castella says.

And Castella can often recall her most memorable skating moments.

"My favorite moment is seeing skaters with a bright smile on their faces talking about how much they love the sport from the many times they have fallen down to the smaller victories in conquering a new skill. I love it when students say 'I love this sport' not just for the tricks but because the lessons they have learned, transcend on an intrapersonal and interpersonal level. Being able to truly understand the power we each have and how we can inspire, motivate and support one another is one of the best moments I have with skaters of all ages."

And it is her students that most inspire this adult skater to be her very best.

"My students inspire me to be authentic, genuine and inspire me to continue working hard within my own skating. It makes me appreciate how despite our differences where we are in life we can come together to learn from one another with the sport of figure skating. My students continue to be an inspiration to be the best version of myself, and forever skate," Castella says.

Heather's Story

"I think the best teachers are the ones who continually learn from their students. Skating keeps me humble and reminds me of the teacher that I want to be for my students"

—Heather Hilgar

For Heather Hilgar, learning and mastering a new skill as an adult skater means a lot. Perhaps because this dedicated lady can visualize just what her very special first graders go through every day.

Heather is a competitive skater and won numerous medals at Adult Championships, and for the past nineteen years, she is a proud first grade teacher.

"I love the first grade personalities," Heather states. "They are so honest and accepting. Skating has been a huge asset to my teaching. The big hurdle in first grade is learning to read. Each child has to find the strategy that works and practice, practice, practice. Doesn't that sound just like skating? I struggled my first months on the ice and continue to struggle today."

According to Heather, struggling is perhaps an understatement. She actually "fell" into figure skating quite by mistake.

Having transferred from another college to the University of Delaware, Heather was one credit short of a requirement for graduation. It was either a PE course (volley ball or figure skating) or a Science course on the Genetic Toxicology of Insecticides.

"It was definitely as difficult as it sounded. It was going to be too much for my course load. I chose ice skating because it was an individual sport and if I was really awful at it, no one would suffer."

Turns out, this adult medalist's first lessons were a disaster.

"Everyone else skated while I held onto the wall," Heather recalls. "Everyone else tried waltz jumps while I stood on two feet willing one of them to leave the ice."

Fortunately, for Heather, class pro Elaine Ahern was patient and encouraging.

"She loved a good challenge. Had she given up on me I would not be where I am now," Heather says.

One day the class learned the classic "Shoot the Duck". This was the first move Heather tried with them, and she guesses she fell about 30 times. Finally, however, she mastered the skill, got over her fear and started to learn other skills like crossovers and turns, with the rest of the group. When it came time to learn jumps, coach Elaine introduced Heather to Pam Welch who helped her to be less self conscious and more willing to try new things.

Today Heather's biggest motivation is setting goals and achieving goals.

"I love to skate," Heather exclaims. "I have tried everything, pairs, ice dancing, synchro and theater on ice just to find more ways to be on the ice." Sounds a bit crazy but her favorite part of skating? Practice time.

"I love to practice elements over and over and eventually see improvement. I enjoy pushing myself and being pushed beyond what I expected I could achieve. I treasure the genuine friendships I have built through skating. Supporting others as they work toward their goals as I work towards mine creates such strong friendship levels."

Competition for this determined young woman was at first the most difficult part of skating. For many years, she participated because it was a way to measure her growth towards a goal.

"I had so much anxiety I would often feel ill and upset before I skated and would beat myself up before I skated and beat myself up over every mistake when I finished," Heather recalls.

Even if she won an event, Heather would still be frustrated with herself for the "mistakes" she made.

"Once at Nationals when I sat berating myself in my head over a train wreck of a program, a judge stopped and firmly said to me 'there is nothing wrong with your skating. You just need to get out of your own head.' Then, finally, it happened. I got out of my own head and this year was the first year I truly enjoyed competition."

Heather credits a combination of a great support system of friends and excellent coaching that pushed her out of her comfort zone and helped her look at competing in a new way.

"Competition has become a way to share my story and my love of skating with others," states now joyful Heather "It's not just about the mistakes, because we all make them. That is what makes us keep coming back. It is about the courage to try even though you may not succeed. Then there are those rare and special moments when everything comes together the way it's supposed to and you touch people in the audience and they get the story you are trying to tell."

Indeed this determined new adult skater did not believe she would ever have a magical moment on the ice, but that was soon to change.

"It was the most wonderful feeling," gushes Heather. "March 2018 was my magical moment at Adult Eastern Sectionals."

The East coast that year happened to have a large number of entrants so they held an initial round and a final round to select the four Championship qualifiers.

"This terrified me because I had a history of skating well the first time and totally messing up the second time," Heather recalls.

For the first round, I actually skated better than I expected. I achieved my new personal best IJS score and won the initial round which qualified me for the final round, making me last to skate!"

Of course worry set in, and Heather was sure she would not be able to skate her program well the second time around.

"Before stepping on the ice I remember telling my coach and Olympian Suzy Semanick-Schurman, 'I am sorry. I never can skate well twice.' She with her usual intense positive energy, which is the only thing stronger than my negative energy, ignored my comment and knew the exact right thing to say at that moment. My final thought before my music started, besides don't hold your breath, was my friends know I love to skate, my coach knows I love to skate but these judges may not know it yet. I have worked hard to improve the quality of my skating and I can't let that go by being worried about elements."

Close friends Debby, Amy and Jane were rink side that day and hugging each other with excitement.

"Then all my fellow skaters and friends came rushing over as the scores were announced. I had achieved another personal best (more than 41 points which was actually a long term goal for me) and had won the event," states a proud Heather.

Heather also shared that moment of celebration with her skating family, her coach and her special friends. She treasures the picture they took together that day because it was taken after that very special moment on ice

"All the frustrations and anxiety were worth it for just that special moment," Heather says. "I am so thankful that I got the chance to be able to experience a moment like that."

Skating has changed this young woman's life in so many ways. Not just on that special day, but every time she is on the ice. It has given her the most special group of skating friends (family really), and even helped with a long time balance disorder.

"I entered skating as a non athlete and managed to find success and a passion that I wouldn't trade for anything. You will have challenges but the feeling of finally meeting them is amazing. You will build friendships with some of the most wonderful people. You will learn so much about yourself. Most importantly, you will have a place. No matter who you are you will have a place in the adult skating community with many amazing, caring people."

This very enthusiastic skater is also proud of the influence skating has had on her special first graders.

"An added benefit is that since first graders always love their teacher, they often do what I am doing. Many have tried skating as a result," states a proud Heater.

When it comes to skating, Heather Hilgar loves everything about her sport.

"I love to practice in the early morning and listen to my favorite music all by myself on the ice. I love the feeling of gaining more power from a single push, increasing speed while in a spin, and landing a jump with flow. I love the challenge of leaning new elements and the comfort of practicing skills over again. I love achieving something I never expected to do. I love being genuinely happy for my friends' success, and they are happy for mine. I love everything about skating and I am so glad skating found me."

Kimberly's Story

"If it wasn't for all the members of Team Kim, I wouldn't have made it through, on and off the ice, all these years. For it is because of them and the memory of my loving skating dad Jim that have kept me skating forward"

–Kimberly Ellsworth-Flores

K imberly Ellsworth-Flores happily looks back on a very blessed childhood. This U.S. Adult Championship medalist from Michigan is grateful for the many wonderful activities growing up such as tennis, piano and flute lessons, drama and musical productions, and of course, skating.

Like many skaters, Kimberly actually began as a roller skater, but after watching the 1988 Olympics featuring the "Battle of the Brians" & "Duel of the Carmens" she told her parents that she had to "do that".

"Shortly after I started group lessons at the Plymouth Cultural Center I then transitioned to private lessons. My first custom ice skating dress was made by Andrea and it was based on Katarina Witt's Carmen dress at the 1988 Olympics," Kimberly says.

While attending the University of Michigan, Kimberly juggled being a full-time student, continuing competitive skating with the University of Michigan Figure Skating Club and being a four year member of the Michigan Marching band in the piccolo section.

After graduation, Kimberly transitioned into adult skating.

"Back then you had to be 25 years old to enter an adult competition," Kimberly explains. "In 2006, I attended my first Adult Nationals in Dallas, TX and medaled. My dad, my travel buddy, drove 2.5 days to Texas so I could compete. We had time to sightsee which was very special because I got to revisit places with my dad from my childhood trips like the Stockyards and South Fork, the house that was the setting for the 1980s show "Dallas". When I was a kid my parents called me 'The Walking TV Guide'."

Those memories, spending time with her dad, mean so much to Kimberly, today, more than ever. Especially since her travel companion and biggest cheerleader is no longer here. It is still a difficult part of her life.

"Competitions were a family affair," Kimberly remembers. "People called mom, dad and me the 'Three Musketeers'. My dad was an amateur photographer and loved taking pictures at skating events."

The time around Memorial Day will always be difficult for Kimberly.

"Not only was my dad a Vietnam Veteran but it was the day after Memorial Day that my dad got the phone call, home alone, that he had an incurable cancer."

The diagnosis came 13 months before Kimberly's wedding day.

"The doctor gave him six months to live. My dad fought hard to the end. He showed such grace and strength through all the chemo treatments and surgeries. My dad walked me down the aisle on my wedding day. Sixteen months later, he passed away. Mom and I had to find our new normal. Holidays are very hard but the daily living without him is the hardest. My parents were high school sweethearts."

When Kimberly's dad passed away, the skating community was wonderful. They were family. The outpouring of phone calls, cards, emails, flowers, gifts and kind words were amazing. Her skating family helped her get through. Many of her skating friends remembered the photo CDs of their competition performances that Kimberly's dad would give them. They missed him doing that kind deed.

"Not only did I lose my dad I lost my buddy and friend," Kimberly sadly recalls. "He was my biggest fan on and off the ice."

After her dad's passing in October 2010, Kimberly found she liked competitions less, shows and exhibitions more. Over time, she actually stopped travelling to competitions.

She also remembers a special event where Kimberly knows her dad served as her inspiration and on ice angel when she performed three times in Skate for Hope, a cancer benefit show.

In 2015, Kimberly decided to venture back to competitions once again when her husband became her new travel buddy. She feels blessed that Atticus is the "Perfect Skating Hubby."

"The highlight of 2016 was my return to Adult Nationals. They were in my home state of Michigan. Friends that hadn't seen me skate in years were able to come watch my Silver Free Skate event." Kimberly recalls.

Even though Kimberly came in fifth she was proud to skate clean to a piece of music, selections from the "Untouchables" soundtrack, that meant so much to her.

"I know my dad was looking down watching me with a huge smile," she says. "I am a big Paul Wylie fan and Chicago gangster history buff. Paul Wylie skated to the "The Untouchables" at the 1993 World Professional Championships."

At Adult Championships in 2008 in Lake Placid, Kimberly skated to "The Untouchables" for the first time and won the pewter medal. It was also a special occasion because her dad was present to watch her medal winning performance.

Revisiting "The Untouchables" program in 2016, at the urging of her longtime coach Tammy Liptak, was therapeutic, and Kimberly found the joy of competitive skating again.

There have been many more magical moments on ice for this special young woman like medaling at two Intercollegiate Nationals, passing adult gold moves and being on the Arctic Figure Skating Club's Junior Team, placing third at Theatre on Ice Nationals.

"There have been so many but if I had to pick one it was my first IJS Season at the 2018 Midwestern Adult Sectionals where I received a Special Achievement Award pin for my Haircutter Spin and I qualified for the Championship Silver Ladies event at Adult Nationals," Kimberly smiles. "It was only my second time trying to qualify for that Championship event. 2018 also marked my tenth time competing at Adult Nationals. I skated to selections from the "Henry V" soundtrack. Paul Wylie skated to "Henry V" at the 1992 Olympics."

Skating and the ice have always been there for Kimberly.

"Boys came and went. Friends came and went. Even when my dad passed away from cancer, the ice was there for me. There were days that skating was the only reason I got out of bed. Even though there was a time where all I could do was cry when I was on the ice," Kimberly explains. "When laid off from my day job of 11 years that paid for my skating, my parents and my husband were determined to help me stay on the ice. They knew how much skating was a part of my life. Skating is a part of my identity."

Kimberly worked as a graphic designer for several years. After a reduction in force layoff, thanks to the encouragement of her longtime coach Tammy Liptak and others, Kimberly began the process to become a Learn to Skate Instructor.

"I remember when I got the clipboard that meant I had my own class and I was on the payroll."

Today she's happy to announce she's been a LTS coach now for several years, has two private students and judges local Basic Skills competitions. In the spring of 2019, Kimberly competed in a Skate Canada event in Ontario placing first. In the fall of 2019, she will compete in her first Adult ISU competition in Lake Placid.

There are many reasons Kimberly Ellsworth-Flores still loves to skate.

"I love the smell of the ice," she says. "Performing is in my blood. Also, I've been skating so long now I'm kind of scared not to have it in my life. I feel like the line from Seal's "Kiss from a Rose" sums it up best. 'You remain my power, my pleasure, my pain'.

If it weren't for all the members of Team Kim, I wouldn't have made it through, on and off the ice, all these years. For it is because of them and the memory of my loving skating dad Jim that have kept me skating forward."

Aleli's Story

"Every time I step onto the ice I am transformed back to my 10 year old self. It's my dream coming into full circle. My inner child who fell in love with the "ice fairies" has become an "ice fairy" herself. I became part of the world of skating, a beautiful sport."

–Aleli Tirados.

A leli Tirados began skating lessons nearly five years ago, at 39 years young.

"I'm currently an Adult 3 and planning to continue competing," announces a proud Aleli. "I have been competing for nearly four years now. My most recent competition was the Pasadena Open on Thursday September 13, 2018."

That date will forever be a memorable one for Aleli. She won first place in the Adult 1-6 Artistic Showcase event.

"Two years ago I placed fourth, also in the Pasadena Open in Basic 3, and felt disappointed. After having heart to heart talks with my coach and skater friends I realized that I needed to rethink my strategy, to concentrate more on my personal progress rather than compare my skating level with other skaters at higher levels."

Born and raised in the Philippines, Aleli fell in love with skating at 10 years old.

"My family and I would watch Holiday on Ice the day after Christmas. I will never forget how the skaters that I called the "ice fairies" performed their wintry dance on the frozen stage. It was a magical and enchanting memory," Aleli recalls.

Sadly, Aleli did not get the chance to learn ice skating since ice rinks were not available at the time considering the tropical weather where she lived.

"If ice skating were there my parents would not allow me or my siblings to even try skating for a day (and most definitely not take lessons). Money was tight and they focused on more important things like education, paying the bills, food and living expenses."

With skating now such a major part of her life, Aleli spends time on ice for exercise and experience.

"Being able to relate and connect with the professional skaters specific feelings like stress from getting pressured to perform your best at competitions etc., and simply to have fun. Sometimes socializing during public sessions where I have the chance to teach basic moves to first timers. It's one of my outlets to overcome my shyness. Eventually, I will be able to perform at shows when the time comes. First there is gaining more confidence, more practice and learning new moves," Aleli says.

This very enthusiastic adult skater will be the first to tell you that skating pretty much changed her life beginning with her first magical moment on ice, her first ISI competition in April 2015.

"I recall not wearing any fancy costume, just a pair of sequined skating pants, a sparkly black long sleeve blouse and black boot covers," remembers Aleli. "I smiled, yet I was a nervous wreck. Yet, I was happy after my very short compulsory moves program for Pre Alpha. I was relieved that I didn't fall down. Although I was the only skater in that event, I won first place, my very first skating medal. I guess reaching my childhood dream of becoming a figure skater is considered as my magical moment."

Skating also taught Aleli many skills that she applies in her life outside the rink.

"I learned and prioritized the importance of a healthy lifestyle," she explains. "I became more active, enjoying dancing, walking, climbing the stairs. I noticed how much we cut down on watching TV and playing computer games. Also, I cook more homemade meals for my family and me. I don't get the urge to buy or takeout fast food anymore. I enjoy eating more fruits and vegetables."

Aleli also works as an Intermediate Typist Clerk with the County of Los Angeles, a job she has held for the past five years. She is also proud to serve as her workplace Wellness Coordinator.

"These skills are very useful when I share them with my coworkers," Aleli continues. "My performance at work is more productive. I learned to organize my items, paperwork, files and manage my time so that I am not stressed out if there are assignments and projects to be finished before the deadline," Aleli says.

Skating also changed Aleli's life in another way. It has, and still does provide the best therapy for this young woman.

"I've had PTSD since childhood. Whenever I skate, I am at peace and calm. The ice rink is my second home and playground. The coolness of the wind brushing up against my face when I glide makes me feel like I am flying even though I am still on the ground or on the ice in this case," she smiles. "One day I will go airborne when I land my first waltz jump. Other girls bullied me because I was an overweight and chubby child. I didn't play sports because I was not very good, even though I tried. I became shy, withdrawn and had few friends until I turned 17 when my family finally migrated to the United States."

She is also a very proud aunt. Her younger brother and sister gifted Aleli with four beautiful nieces, the youngest just three years old and a twenty two year old nephew. She also treasures her two cats, two dogs and three goldfish. Activities off ice keep her busy as well.

"When I'm not skating I am strength training at the 24 hour fitness center at least twice a week. As a music lover I love to sing and dance and belong to two dance groups, the Los Angeles Zombies (Thrill the World LA) and Zumba Halftime who perform at the Staples Center during the Sparks and Clippers Games."

She also participated in ballroom, hula and Filipino folk dance.

"I love the idea of connecting skating, and dancing considering how similar they are in many ways. The only difference is that skating is a more challenging dance that requires special shoes with skinny steel blades. My adult skating friends call them "knife shoes", and your dance floor is more slippery," Aleli laughs.

Aleli also likes to encourage other adults to give this very special sport a try.

"First I would share this quote by CS Lewis. 'You are never too old to set another goal or to dream a new dream'. In my case I'm living my childhood dream," Aleli encourages.

She also notes that her encouragement came from a very special skater and now dear friend, and coach, Michael Christian Martinez. Michael competed at the Socci and Pyeonchang Olympics representing the Philippines.

"Even though he didn't medal he continues to inspire others that it's not impossible to reach a dream. It takes faith, heart and pure determination. I am fully aware of the great risk in adult skating. Then again, there is no such thing as a risk free life. Sometimes one must go out of their comfort zone. I have heard sayings like 'take a leap of faith'. I would probably ask 'how will you know you can't skate if you don't try?' It's true it is terrifying because it's not natural, in the beginning."

To be honest, Aleli still gets scared when skating. Slips and fall in practice can happen even if she takes extra care.

"But then I learned to anticipate the movement of the other skaters, whether they are experienced or not. I also learned that skaters of all ages and levels do fall. Falling is a part of the package of figure skating. What matters is that you get up and try again. When I competed at my first Pacific Coach Sectionals, I was simply amazed that there were many skaters older than I was. I even made friends with them. I felt I wasn't too old after all. I was relieved that I wasn't alone, knowing there are others who love and are living their dreams of figure skating regardless of age, gender, faith and nationality."

For Aleli Tirados, skating gives her many blessings, and she feels grateful it's a part of her life. In February 2019, Aleli saw another dream come true. She served as a volunteer for the ISU Four Continents competition in Anaheim, CA and worked among many of her skating idols.

"Whenever I skate I can be myself. I can have fun and be creative. There's an enchanting feeling when the blades curve the ice. I feel strong and passionate by expressing the story of my life through my choice of music," Aleli explains. "I realized that a figure skater is a combination of athlete, actor and artist. The smooth ice is like a blank canvas and the blades carve out intricate lobes, curves and swirls. Every time I step onto the ice, I'm transformed back to my 10 year old self. It's my dream, coming into full circle. My inner child who fell in love with the "ice fairies" has become an "ice fairy" herself. I became a part of the world of skating, a beautiful sport."

Christine's Story

"It's when they let you into their world and trust you. They allow me to be a goof, and we celebrate all the milestones"

–Christine Crowe

Many adult skaters spend hours on the ice perfecting their skills, readying themselves for competitions, test sessions and exhibitions. Many adult skaters also spend hours on the ice sharing their talent with young up and coming skaters. Christine Crowe is one of those adult skaters.

Christine Crowe is an USFS adult bronze skater and ISI-FS4 and Open Silver skater. She also proudly teaches Learn to Skate classes at the Ice Factory in Kissimmee, FL and she happily admits her Learn to Skate classes are Fun, Fun, Fun!

Christine loves to make her little ones class an interesting one and she has the tools to do it.

"Stuffed animals, markers and a pool noodle," Christine explains. "My pool noodle has been a popular tool with all levels."

Christine is one enthusiastic skating pro, but she will be the first to tell you her students inspire her to be a better skater.

"My students remind me to take it back to the basics and work on my mechanics," Christine admits. "So many times we forget the fundamentals while we prepare to compete and the key to a safe and successful program begins with the basics. Now when I warm up I go through my list of all elements."

Anyone who witnesses Christine's classes knows they are in for a lot of fun while learning the basics of skating.

"I am known as the Cone-Head Coach," Christine laughs. "I put a Learn to Skate Cone through my ponytail and the rest is history. Creating memories, celebrating and having fun. Throwing in a bit of showgirl with my classes has been fun. The little girls are butterflies, the little boys, superheroes."

And Christine loves to use tricks to teach little ones the mechanics of skating.

"Bubbles are fun," she exclaims, "I have the kids go step step boogie shake boogie shake… and try to catch the bubbles on their nose." Using Crayola terms in speak that the kids can connect with helps create a great balance-along with fun music!"

For this special coach, teaching her students in a unique, special way is what she loves most about teaching skating.

"For the little ones, it's when they let you into their world and trust you. They allow me to be me, and we celebrate the milestones. For the teens and adults, it's when they quit thinking and have that AH HA moment," Christine says.

Looking forward. Just days before her 55th birthday, Christine suffered a stroke, which affected her left side. Testing her USFS adult gold moves put on hold while her focus is on Turbo Rehab. Christine's 2019/2020 goals are set! Take and pass her gold moves and compete at the Winter World Masters Games in Innsbruck, Austria.

There is little doubt this special coach and adult skater will indeed accomplish these treasured goals.

Kimberly's Story

"Skating will carry me through a musical slump, and music will carry me through a skating slump. The best times are when both are on a glorious high waiting for the next fun performance, or the next new skating skill to learn"

–Kimberly Coxe

Meet Kimberly Coxe, one very busy adult skater who at the age of 34 began her ice journey. In a very short time, this Cleveland skater achieved her adult gold moves, and bronze freestyle and dance. She's also competed in several competitions around the world.

You might also see this talented lady, however, playing as a woodwind specialist in stage musical productions throughout the Cleveland area.

"My degrees from college are in BM Music Education and MM in Music performance Woodwind Specialist," Kimberly says.

In fact, during her college years, her talent brought her to play in her first musicals, *Damn Yankees* and *She Loves Me*. In 2000 back in Cleveland, Kimberly hooked up with the music scene and found not just the orchestral music scene was alive and thriving but the community and touring theater scene too.

"I perform in 6 to 12 musical a year so if you have heard of the musical I just might have performed it," states a proud Kimberly. "My favorite answer for what instruments do you play is 'What are you hiring for'? The real answer is the family of instruments including clarinets, saxophone, oboes and bassoon! I don't play bassoon much anymore, but I do get regularly hired with the rest!"

Kimberly has played in 70 musicals, many of them several times. With a list that long, she definitely has her favorites!

"My favorites have been *Les Miserable* because of the quality of the high school cast and the musical was just outstanding," she recalls. "*The Secret Garden*, because the first reed book calls for 13 instruments. I have never had so many instruments around me that I needed to know how to play at the same TIME."

Other favorites include the *Children of Eden* because of the beautiful story of the father son relationship. "It also has some lovely music and of course, any show my husband and I get to play together."

Yes, Kimberly's husband David is in the pit playing piano or directing.

"Makes for some fun family time," she says.

This talented young woman is just as passionate about her other love, besides music. Skating, of course.

Kimberly began skating at the age of 34, thinking it would be a fun place to cool off in the summer and more exercise than going to the gym!

"I started skating at Learn to Skate at Winterhurst in Lakewood where I coach group lessons now," Kimberly explains. "I am a club member at Pavilion Skating Club of Cleveland Heights where I practice and take some private lessons on Sundays."

She also practices and teaches private lessons at the North Olmstead Recreation Center, takes her own lessons at Winterhurst and sometimes even finds herself at the Cleveland Skating Club and Shaker Heights Ice Rink. If skating calls, this determined adult skater will be there.

"My most memorable years have been when I won the Pre Bronze Dance and my pewter for Light Entertainment at Adult Nationals," Kim remembers. She also took a sabbatical from work to compete and tour in New Zealand and Australia with her husband David.

Today she is happily competing and coaching, and chairs the Buckeye Adult Open. Recently she brought home pewter and silver medals from the 2019 Adult Championships, in Freestyle and Solo Dance, a very proud moment for Kimberly.

She also finds skating and performing in musicals have many similarities.

"They both have fundamentals to be learned," she explains. "I have found that skating moves in the field and figures are very similar to learning and practicing scales on an instrument. They are a foundational skill and can be repeated over and over to make you better at your craft."

Auditioning is also very similar to testing.

"The ability to know you have prepared, you are ready and know what you have to present is very much the same mental game. Then there is actually performing while you are nervous. Just go out there and trust your training. This is the same for music and performing in the pit. You know what you are doing, prove it every time!"

Finally, Kimberly sees competing is much like the actual musical event.

"You know you are ready. You know you will make mistakes," she says. "It's how you cover those mistakes and continue on to sell the whole performance that counts. Musicians in the pit all know I skate and they often ask what it is like and I tell them it can feel very much the same from the frustration of a bad performance to the glory and excitement of your most perfect performance to date."

This very accomplished musician still has a dream or two she would love to achieve, and that dream is to someday play Broadway.

"While a stage actor always dreams to be on Broadway or in a movie, for me to play in the pit or for a movie soundtrack would be the ultimate use of my talents and so much fun," adds Kimberly.

For Kimberly Coxe the most important aspect is love of the event.

"If you don't love skating why keep doing it?" Kimberly says. "The same goes for music. You have to love it to continue doing it."

Kimberly admits there were times when she had to take a step back in both her skating and music to reevaluate her mental readiness. But once this determined young woman decides she is willing to continue it is Game On!

"Get me back up on the ice and back in the practice room," Kimberly exclaims. "In this way, the mental games are so attached. I am happiest when the slumps for either do not line up. Skating will carry me through a musical slump and music will carry me through a skating slump. The best times are when both are on a glorious high waiting for the next fun performance or the next new skill to learn."

Terryl Lee's Story

"These medals are thrown on the ice for the skater out of respect, as encouragement for effort in the face of great resistance or struggle and for support."

–Terryl Lee Allen

T he scenario is most unusual, but it is true. Adult skaters at the U.S. Adult Championships love to get medals, and the ones they treasure most are created by and given to them by a fellow former adult skater Terryl Lee Allen. Once an adult International competitor (Oberstdorf, Germany) and Adult Championship competitor, today her adult skater friends know Terryl as the lovely lady who creates the spectacular "tossie" medals she presents at the event each year.

"The tossie medals were the result of trying to find small tossies that could be carried to the ISU competition (in Germany)," Terryl says.

Tossies, as anyone who attends an adult competition knows, are very popular with skaters. Nearly every skater brings them along to toss to their fellow skaters to encourage them after each skate. Tossies range from stuffed animals, candy, flowers and anything in between.

And then there are Terryl's medals.

"The first ones were stock medals with a card that said 'For your passion to skate and your courage to compete.' It occurred to me I should design my own medals because I really wanted the medal to reflect adult skating and adult skaters. So I did just that. I create the design and have a company produce the actual medal."

Terryl's first experience on the ice was at age 13 in Switzerland. Her father was on sabbatical to the University of Zurich. His birth place. A former hockey player, he decided there was ice, so his daughters would skate. He found used figure skates for the each daughter, and Terryl still remembers her special brown skates.

"That winter my sisters and I lived at the outdoor rink," Terryl recalls. "My dad coached a youth hockey team. His team won the league that year and I found a passion for skating. Even though I had no instruction on ice and knew there was no ice back home I begged to bring my skates back to the USA, but no there was not enough room to bring them back home."

Fast forward 26 years and Terryl married and moved to Albuquerque, NM.

"There was a rink! And I began taking lessons at 39+ years old. The rest is history."

Terryl's motivation to skate comes from how difficult it is to actually accomplish anything in this very difficult sport.

"I have zero natural talent on the ice and had to struggle to learn even the most basic skills," Terryl says. "I love the challenge and the process of learning and mastering edges, jumps and spins. "

Terryl began competing as a way to set her goals. Of course, she wanted to win but not as much as she wanted to challenge and test herself.

"This was very useful approach for me as I struggled with several surgeries that impacted my ability to skate such that I could no longer be competitive," Terryl continues.

Terryl continued to skate and enjoyed every second of the process very much until her final season.

"It then became apparent I could no longer skate safely due to a bone issue in my ankle. There is no surgical or therapy repair that does not have serious negative outcome so I have hung up my skates. I continue to volunteer at my local skating club board, serve on the US Figure Skating Adult Skating Committee and attend the US Adult Championships and the ISU Adult championships in Oberstdorf, Germany as a cheerleader."

Then there is the beautiful medal she "tosses" yearly to her fellow competitors. Each design, thoughtfully planned, and Terryl can remember each year's medal and the message it brought. She simply follows four simple rules when creating each design.

Terryl's rules are simple. The medal has a cutout space to represent things yet to accomplish or places in the heart that hold a void created by past events or a place waiting to fill.

The medal must have a connection to figure skating represented in the design in some way. For example, this can be through a blade tracing, a figure skating boot, a figure skating blade or through the representation of the ice.

The design must tell a story inspired by skating, figure skaters or people close to a skater or skating.

Each medal will include the words "For your passion to skate and your courage to compete." These words are the soul of the adult skating world.

Over the years, many "little background facts" came to be part of Terryl's medals.

2008 marked the first year of Terryl's own designs.

"I have an awards company, Crown Awards, who makes the medals from the camera ready art I create," she explains.

Terryl began with 150 medals. That number has now grown to 275.

"I can't afford anymore. About 2/3's of the medals come to the US Adult Nationals and 1/3 go to the ISU Adult Championships in Obertsdorf."

Medals are not limited to skaters.

"I have included other people too. These people are coaches, judges, referees, local organizing committee members and absent skaters who had to skip events due to financial difficulty, schedule conflicts, illness or injury to themselves or in their families," Terryl declares. "This way these people can be included in events they miss because life got in the way."

One thing she won't do is include her name on the tossie medal.

"Until the 2013 design these tossies were pretty much anonymous," laughs Terryl. "But the word got out as to who was throwing the medal tossies so I was not so anonymous anymore."

Each and every medal from the year 2008 to the present is special to Terryl and the skaters who received them. Terryl can happily explain the story behind each medal, and the reason that particular year she chose that design.

The 2008 medal was inspired by the winter Olympics medals from Turin, Italy. Terryl loved these Olympic medals and was thrilled that Tanith Belbin and Benjamin Agosto won the silver medal in ice dancing that year, the best Olympic placement for U.S ice dancing. The Olympic medals that year had a void in the center of the medal to represent the town center plaza and the empty center was to rest over the heart of the wearer. In Terryl's design, the void in the center held the image of the toe of a figure skating boot and skate blade. The boot and blade centered in the void to represent the hopes, dreams, joys and pain of figure skating.

"Learning and practice are often motivated by setting goals. In my case the goals were set and tested by rising to the challenge of reaching for success by meeting previously set goals under the pressure of a competition," Terryl proudly explains.

The 2009 medal Terryl simply titled "Stained Glass". The roots of figure slating's school figures inspired this medal, from what were the "special figures." The overall design was a special figure skated by Nikoli Panin during the 1908 Olympic games. Panin won the 1908 Olympic gold medal for special figures. The shades of blue in the medal represent colors of ice.

"The design also looks very much like stained glass and relates to stained glass in church windows," Terry comments. "Thus the medal is like skating as religion, or source of well being, support and a way to cope and move forward."

In 2010, Terryl introduced the "River of Life" medal. This design is sad. During 2010, two special friends passed away from very rare diseases. They were far too young to pass away and both left behind families and countless friends whose lives they touched with joy and passion.

Both women were powerful inspiring and motivational forces in their lives and respective sports. One was Terryl's best friend Jody Hurlburt who was passionate in Artistic and Rhythmic Gymnastics, the same sport Terryl coached at one time. The other was Paula Smart who was one of the pioneers and energetic advocates for the development of adult skating in the USA.

"There was a skating boot for Paula and a ribbon symbol for Jody," Terryl describes. "The ribbon symbol is there for the Rhythmic Gymnastics ribbon apparatus and it holds the shape of a figure skating figure loop for skating and is the shape of a remembrance ribbon. The color is black for grief and loss. The medal is antique gold finish to remind one to look forward despite the grief. Both these women were bright and full of energy. Pass it forward."

Terryl notes creating the "Phoenix" in 2011 because it represented what was a difficult year for many of her adult skater friends.

"The phoenix or firebird is symbols of hope, rebirth and triumph over hardship. They also hold mystical qualities. The colors are red and orange on brightly polished gold for energy and empowerment. The medal is designed for inspiration and for positive and rewarding outcomes," Terryl describes.

2012 saw the creation of "The Abstract Pond". It was another tough year for Terryl as she lost her dad that year. He played and coached hockey. Terryl was able to compete again that year after a hip surgery.

"That year was an intense mixture of very great things and very hard things," Terryl remembers. "The design was created using four special figures to represent an abstract outdoor meadow and pond for my dad's love of nature and to remember my dad. The colors were bright to represent the positive things in life. The pond was of course for skating in winter. The meadow and pond in this design were in the spring to represent the hope and growth in the New Year after the hard times of winter."

Terryl titled her 2013 medal "The World". It was also the year word got out where the tossie medals came from.

"Until now these medals were thrown anonymously," Terryl says. "A few friends knew who the tosser was but most recipients had no way of knowing where the medals came from. That was about to change."

One skater posted the question on her Facebook page, "Whoever tossed the lovely medal with the pretty purple ribbon to me-thank you. I will cherish it."

That post opened the door and it was no longer a secret. Terryl was officially the proud tosser.

"I have been amazed and humbled beyond words by the comments and responses from skaters who received medals not only this year but from past years," says a humble Terryl. "There was so much meaning in so many of the comments that this year the design is one to say "pass it forward around the world."

The world is the central part of the design. The design also connects each person through the choice of metallic enamel colors to symbolize the testing of one's mettle, an intended pun by use of mettle vs. metal.

"Adult skating is truly a test of a skater's ability to find time to skate, to survive the process of training and overcome the challenges faced in the pursuit of skating and competing from every possible direction," Terryl says. "The dove is for hope that through the testing of one's mettle the skater will be at peace with the outcome of the test."

"Celebration" was the theme for 2014, and one of Terryl's most intricate designs.

"2014 marked the 20th year of the US Adult Championships and the 10th year of the ISU International competition, and it was also an Olympic year. This made the concept of the idea easy. Celebration," Terryl exclaims.

The design, meant to celebrate the ice and how adult figure skating developed over the years. The colors chosen for the ice were white and blue. Glitter is first as a design element, added to the ice for sparkle."

The medal was also silver, which was also a first. The silver medal stood for the saying every cloud has a silver lining.

Terryl also wanted to include a snowflake.

"The snowflake always forms six perfect sides. As adult skaters, we've been or are currently judged on the 6.0 judging system. In skating, as with snowflakes, six is perfection," Terryl replies.

But not one snowflake is the same nor is any individual skater the same. Even though all adult skaters skate, the reasons they skate, how they train, where they train, how long they train, when they begin training, what level of ability they have all contribute to different environments like snowflakes. Each adult skater is different even within the rules and elements of skating.

The center of the medal is the ice surface of the skating rink. She also placed a crystal stone representing the sparkly skating costume.

There is also a heart shape of three dots in the bottom middle representing the love and fun of skating without rules, required elements or competition, and finally the dots between the upper border and center represent clumps of snowflakes falling from the sky, but also flowers in the form of a bouquet.

"Flowers have a tradition of being thrown on the ice in appreciation of a valued performance," adds Terryl. Flowers were one of the first "tossies".

2015's theme revolved around the proverb "Every Cloud has a Silver Lining."

"The proverb means never feel hopeless because difficult times always lead to better days," Terryl says. "Difficult times are like dark clouds that pass overhead and block the sun. It is always possible to get something positive out of a situation no matter how unpleasant difficult or even painful it might seem. Every bad situation has an element of good."

The proverb is encouragement to the person who is overcome by some difficulty and unable to see a positive way forward. This proverb expresses a positive and hopeful attitude about painful or difficult experiences and circumstances. It also describes figure skating very well.

"Adult skaters use the ice as their silver lining," states a proud Terryl. "They also pass on encouragement and support to others. So this design, the medal, is of course silver, but not bright silver, rather darkened or antique silver for those clouds. But through the passion to skate, we know the promise of bright silver with all its sparkle and shine, thus the design also has glitter.

Terryl chose a labyrinth design for 2016.

A labyrinth unlike a maze always allows one to find the center and return without becoming lost. All one needs to do is to continue forward and the center will be found. Likewise, to return one must continue forward from the center and the exit will be found.

"Skating is often used like a labyrinth to help cope, problems solve, reflect and meditate on life beyond skating itself," Terryl reflects. "I find this fascinating because the physical part of skating is more like a maze then a labyrinth.

Sometimes it seems a skill is learned then disappears. One never knows when the skill will be completed how long it takes before it disappears. To help with the path to learning use the guide stick that came with this medal to trace the medal inward as you think of the goals you have before you skate. Take your goals to the ice. When you leave the ice, begin your journey from the center of the labyrinth medal and reflect on your successes and areas of improvement. Perhaps the labyrinth medal can help master the physical skills you wish to learn."

In 2017, it was a song from the group Coldplay that was Terryl's inspiration.

"When you've tried your best and don't succeed. It is heartbreaking for me to see skaters leave the ice filled with joy, satisfaction and triumph at competing a personal best performance only to have evaluation of a judging panel erase the accomplishment and replace it with disappointment, frustration, anger and loss of confidence by receiving a low placement. Even if it is such a placement is appropriate given the skater's performance, it is a crushing blow to passion and courage," acknowledges Terryl.

The skater is the inspiration for this medal design because at some point they tried their best but did not succeed. The tossie, meant to hold, so the reflection of the skate's eye shows in the inner circle of the heart.

"Look into your eyes and into your heart," offers Terryl. "Believe with all your heart and soul that if your tried your best and skated your best, this is the true definition of success. Believe it. And remember always, you are so much more than a podium finish."

The 2018 medal was extra special, for Terryl and for her fellow adult skaters. The title of the medal "We are Family", and it was inspired by the support shown to a skater who qualified for a championship event at the 2017 US Adult Championships in Wake Forest, NC.

"The skater was apprehensive about attending this event due to the political situation in North Carolina that had a number of skaters choosing not to attend in protest," Terryl explains. "With encouragement this skater did attend the competition as so deserved by qualifying to compete."

The support for this skater was fierce. This is what the adult skating family does. Four months later Terryl found out she was no longer able to skate because of a bone alignment problem that made skating extremely unsafe.

The support Terryl received is still powerfully emotional and deeply appreciated.

"Again this is what the adult skating family does," she says. "There is continuing stories of support throughout the adult skating community. Despite the vast differences in the members of our family, this family manages to find ways to support each other. This support is what makes this so unique, so powerful and so rewarding. I hope our family can always offer such meaningful support and keep our hearts open."

And the beautiful 2018 medal of many colors reflects this.

2019 will be the last custom tossie medal Terryl will design. Without consciously doing so, she did not have any skating related elements. The water in this design is liquid, not ice, and the words along the border are not obvious. Even though she no longer skates, Terryl will always have the experiences and memories of her years as a skater, countless friendships established through skating, and she will always have her skating family! So this design, both intentionally and self consciously is a farewell to her skating but not a goodbye to her skating friends and family.

"For the 25th Adult Figure Skating Championships the medal had to be silver and because this will be the last design. Every competitor will receive a tossie medal in his or her goodie bag. The medal design is titled "You Matter," Terryl explains.

The card with the medal reads as follows:

'To everything, there is a season.

My "ice" has melted, I move forward to different passions. This medal will be my last.

YOU MATTER. Your actions, your words, you matter. Your opinion of yourself matters.

Be cognizant that you have impact in the world. Strive to uplift and pass forward kindness and caring.

There is no Planet "B"

These medals, like her love for skating, are a part of Terryl.

"A medal is usually awarded to those who have been declared winners through competition based on time, distance, points or judgments," Terryl says. "In the case of the tossie medals the medal is given to those whose performance inspired, or created an emotional response for a performance that was not what the skater wanted, despite giving great effort in the attempt, to a skater who did not have a tossie other than a tossie medal. These medals are thrown on the ice for the skater out of respect and as encouragement, for effort in the face of great resistance or struggle, and for support. These medals are about the process, not the end result"

Melissa's Story

"I absolutely love when my theater world and skating world collide. Having a deep knowledge of musical theater has opened the door to a large repertoire of music for my skaters that others may not even know exist. The two really go hand in hand"

–Melissa Schamburek

Melissa Schamburek's high school junior year was a banner one in many ways. It was that year that Melissa began skating.

"I actually started skating my junior year of high school," Melissa explains. "Too old to be a 'kid' skater, and still too young to take advantage of US Figure Skating's adult skating opportunities."

So Melissa tested pre- preliminary and preliminary prior to turning 25 ,then tested and passed adult pre- bronze moves and freestyle, and adult bronze moves and freestyle on the SAME day after turning age 25, which was the minimum age to compete as an adult at the time.

"My goal was to pass those tests so I could compete at Adult Nationals in Chicago that year, 2003-and I did! I also competed in Adult Nationals in 2007," Melissa says.

Junior year was also a banner year for another passion that came into Melissa's life. Musical theater. Musical theater still has a "starring" role in her life today.

"I actually started doing musical theater around the same time I started skating, in my later years of high school. I really don't know remember what pushed me to my first audition to be honest. I had friends in theater and I guess I thought it would be fun to spend my summer with them and do a show. My first couple of experiences was really great (they ALL have been) and I was officially hooked."

Melissa also participated in her school choir since early junior high and first exposed to the musical theater repertoire while a choir member.

"It was fun to put together a full show," she fondly remembers. "We are lucky enough today to have a restored vaudeville theater in our town and most of my shows today have been performed on that stage. I love the entire process, but nothing beats taking your bows to the applause and if we're lucky a standing ovation at the end of a show."

Melissa is proud to recount the numerous shows and roles she's played.

"My first role was as a secretary in *How to Succeed in Business without Really Trying*," Melissa remembers. "That was followed by my very favorite show that I have ever done,

Joseph and the Amazing Technicolor Dreamcoat where I played Levi's wife."

That role pushed Melissa's dance skills to the limit, but was so rewarding when it all came together. Many, many people auditioned for that show and Melissa felt honored that someone so new to the stage won the role as one of the twelve wives.

Another favorite role was Shirley Markowicz in *The Producers.*

"I shared that scene with two of my best friends who played Roger and Carmen and I was the lone female in the "Keep it Gay" number."

Other favorite shows include *Chicago, Spring Awakening and A Chorus Line* where she played Vicki.

"Most recently I just finished my first paid job, a ten performance run as Sister Lee in *Do Black Patent Leather Shoes Really Reflect Up?*

The show included 10 performances and was Melissa's longest running show to date.

Melissa also finds that surprisingly many skating skills help her in her theatrical performances.

"Well, I am NOT a dancer. So I find that skating has helped give me the grace that I need on stage that I never got from a dance class. Skating has also given me a sense of musicality to help catch on to show choreography faster" Melissa states.

Melissa's interest in musical theater has given her ideas for showcase numbers for her Learn to Skate classes, and helps with her ice show choreography.

"For example, a group of my students did a small entertainment number last season to "I Know it's Today" from *Shrek* and I was assistant coach to a large ensemble production number based on *Newsies*."

After performing in many shows, Melissa still finds the audition process intimidating, but encourages anyone who has always dreamed of being on stage to give it a try.

"Nine times out of ten the people running the auditions much like skating judges WANT you to succeed and will gently guide you through the audition and if you get cast it is so worth the risk. You'll make lifelong friends, tons of memories and broaden your artistic horizons

Always choose an audition song that highlights your strong points as well as fits into the character of the show. It is generally not advised to audition with a song from the show your auditioning for."

One more piece of advice.

"Try and steer clear from the cliché, over used audition pieces," advises Melissa. "That list, by the way can be found with a quick Google search."

Today Melissa continues to enjoy coaching her Learn to Skate classes, private lessons and Beginner 2 synchro team, and she does look forward to competing in skating one day in the future when life slows down a bit. Skating, theater and being the mom of three little girls who also skate take up the hours in most of Melissa's days.

Still this dedicated performer has that one show she still dreams of performing in one day. *Mamma Mia.*

"It was just released for Community Theater licensing so I am keeping my fingers crossed that we do it next season," states a hopeful Melissa. "I grew up listening to Abba music on summer road trips when I was a kid, so I've always loved their music."

Melissa is a great fan of the stage show, and saw both movies numerous times.

"Every time I've seen it I left feeling so energized and inspired, and I am ready to tackle it on stage. My stretch goal is the role of Tanya, but I would be so happy just in the chorus."

Mostly, this young mom, coach and musical theater performer enjoys blending her two favorite worlds. Skating and theater.

"I absolutely love when my theater world and skating world collide," Melissa says. "Having a deep knowledge of musical theater has opened the door to a large repertoire of music for my skaters that others may not even know exist. The two really go hand in hand."

PHOTO CREDITS

Suzie Marie Flynn – Photo by Gregg Mokrzycki

Tracy Blomquist – Photo by Tracy Blomquist

Ken Ho – Photo by Robert Killmer

Karen Viel – Photo by US Figure Skating 2013 US Adult Championships

Castella Copeland – Photo by RES Video and Media 2019 Eastern Adult Sectionals

Heather Hilgar – Photo by Heather Hilgar

Kimberly Ellsworth-Flores – Photo by Kristin Godfrey

Aleli Tirados –Photo by Aleli Tirados

Christine Crowe – Photo by Christine Crowe

Kimberly Coxe – Photo by Kimberly Coxe

Terryl Lee Allen – Photo by Terryl Lee Allen

Melissa Schamburek – Photo by Melissa Schamburek

Made in the USA
Middletown, DE
01 March 2020

85613821R00061